PRAISE FOR *My Favorite Color Is Blue. Sometimes.*

"Our world is increasingly rediscovering that grief and trauma are whole-body experiences. Hutchison's imagery and art are a feast for the eyes, soaking into the mind's memories and rendering fresh tears, smiles, and that human-divine alchemy of prayer that all great art performs.

—TROY BRONSINK, founder of The Hive: A Center for Contemplation, Art, and Action and author of *Drawn In: A Creative Process for Artists, Activists, and Jesus Followers.*

"This original volume belongs in every collection of books for children about grief."

—WENDY MOGEL, PHD, *New York Times* bestselling author of *The Blessing of a Skinned Knee*

"*My Favorite Color Is Blue. Sometimes.* Is a fabulous book. For all ages. All you need to appreciate it are feelings and a love of colors."

—GAIL GODWIN, *New York Times* bestselling author of *Father Melancholy's Daughter*

"Through brilliant colors revealed and remembered, Roger offers sacred space to dwell with grief and be at peace."

—LISA KIMBALL, PHD, Virginia Theological Seminary

"Roger Hutchison's *My Favorite Color Is Blue. Sometimes.* explores the many colors of bereavement and invites the reader to paint a picture of the memories and emotions that make up their personal grief journey."

—MARIAN MANKIN, Program Director of Bo's Place, Houston, TX

"Roger Hutchison takes you on a beautiful pilgrimage through sadness, grief, joy and remembrance."

—SASHA MCLEAN, LMFT, LPC, Executive Director of Archway Academy, Houston, TX

"Working in hospice and palliative care, we often discussed the lack of appropriate resources to help the children, grandchildren, and siblings of our patients process their grief. I wish I'd had a copy of *My Favorite Color Is Blue. Sometimes.* on my shelf."

—SARAH H. CROSS, LMSW, MPH

Dedicated to those who color my world . . .
God, the creator of all color.
The children and families I serve each day.
My family and friends.
This book is also dedicated to those I have loved whose
memories live on in the colors of a shooting star or
the deep blue of a summer sky.
Thank you for reminding me that you
are always with me.

My Favorite Color Is Blue.
Sometimes.

A Journey
Through
Loss
with Art
and Color

ROGER HUTCHISON

PARACLETE PRESS
BREWSTER, MASSACHUSETTS

2018 Second Printing
2017 First Printing

My Favorite Color Is Blue. Sometimes.: A Journey Through Loss with Art and Color

Copyright © 2017 by Roger Hutchison

ISBN 978-1-61261-923-1

The Paraclete Press name and logo (dove on cross) are trademarks of Paraclete Press, Inc.

Library of Congress Cataloging-in-Publication Data

    Names: Hutchison, Roger, author.
    Title: My favorite color is blue, sometimes : a journey through loss with art
      and color / Roger Hutchison.
    Description: Brewster, Massachusetts : Paraclete Press Inc., 2017.
    Identifiers: LCCN 2017028004 | ISBN 9781612619231 (trade paper)
    Subjects: LCSH: Color--Psychological aspects. | Loss (Psychology)
    Classification: LCC BF789.C7 H88 2017 | DDC 242/.4--dc23
    LC record available at https://lccn.loc.gov/2017028004

10 9 8 7 6 5 4 3 2

Published by Paraclete Press
Brewster, Massachusetts
www.paracletepress.com

Printed in the United States of America

My Favorite Color Is Blue.

Sometimes.

My favorite color is blue.
Sometimes.
Blueberries taste sweet. I eat them by the handful.
I like looking up at the bright blue sky and sticking
    my toes into the deep blue of the sea.
Bluebonnets are flowers that dance in the breeze.
Sometimes I wonder if they fell from the sky.

Blue is my favorite color.
Just not today.
Today I feel blue—the swirling blue of a rainstorm.
The storm is inside of me.
I am angry.
I am sad.
My heart is hurting.

6

Love is red.

Anger is red, too.

When I heard that you were gone, I felt a
flash inside of me and I felt like I could
not breathe. My ears felt hot. My
stomach tightened.

I love you.

I'm angry with you, too.

Why did you go away?

I miss you.

Love is red...
and I really love you.

Blue mixed with red makes purple.
Purple is quiet.
Purple listens.
Purple remembers.
I remember
　　　your eyes,
　　　　　　your laughter.
I remember so many things about you.
Remembering makes it easier to breathe.
I take a deep breath.
Remembering makes me smile.

Black is the smell of coffee.

Black is the silent night sky.

Black is finding a dark hiding place when playing
hide-and-go-seek with your friends.

Some people are afraid of the dark.

You taught me to not be afraid.

Black is my room when it is time to fall asleep.

Black are the scribbles on a page when I don't
know what else to draw or write.

Black is the shadow on my wall.

Black is sometimes feeling very small.

It's hard right now to not be afraid,

but I think of you and I feel strong.

Black is being brave.

You taught me to be brave.

13

When I think of you
    I see yellow.
Yellow is the flickering flame of a candle.
Yellow is a sour lemon.
Yellow is a sunflower
    standing tall and proud.
Yellow is a soft blanket,
    comfort on a cold morning.
Yellow is holding hands.
Yellow is a shooting star in the night sky.
You blink and it is gone.

You are a shooting star.
Your light trails across the heavens.
I blinked
    and you were gone.

Brown is warm dirt
    in a summer garden.
Brown is the old penny I found on the sidewalk.
Brown is the tall tree I like to climb.
Brown is the silence of autumn leaves
    floating in the breeze.
Brown is the color of my sweet dog.
She licks my face and I laugh.

YOU always made me laugh!
Even with tears in my eyes, thinking of you
  makes me laugh!
Brown is the color of telling stories,
    and I want to tell everyone about you.

White is the moon hanging low in the evening sky
keeping watch as we dream.

White is the swirling wind.

White is snow falling softly on winter ground.

White is sometimes empty.

I'm feeling kind of empty right now.

White is the sand on the beach.

White is the sound of the ocean crashing at my
feet.

White is listening for the voice that speaks in a
whisper.

White is knowing that you will always be with me.

Orange are the leaves on
an autumn tree.
Orange is the pumpkin
with a crooked smile.
Orange is the swoosh of
a basketball through
the net.
Orange is cheerful and
strong.
Orange is the sweet taste
of a persimmon.
Orange is swinging from
the monkey bars at
the playground.
Orange is strumming the
strings of a guitar.
Orange is exciting and
full of imagination.
Orange is wise.
You were so very wise.

Green is a promise.
Green is new life.
Green is planting seeds and watching them grow.
Green are the stems of the flowers that make me
   think of you.
Green are the fields where we played together.
Green are the leaves of our favorite tree dancing in
   the breeze.
Green is tilling the soil.
Green is the changing of seasons.
Green is learning to trust.
Green is filled with hope.
Green is a new beginning.
Oh how I miss you. I always will.

22

Blue is my favorite color.

But so is
Red

and

Purple

and

Black

and

Yellow

and
Brown

and
White

and
Orange

and
Green!

These are all my favorite colors
because each one of them
makes me think of . . .

YOU!

Ways to Remember and Celebrate
the Life of your Loved One

- Draw a picture of their smiling face.
- Write a story about something you loved doing with them.
- Plant a tree in their memory.
- Make a scrapbook using some of your favorite photos or memorabilia.
- Prepare their favorite meal and share it with friends or take it to a shelter to share with the hungry.
- Celebrate their life through a worship service or vigil.
- Remember them in your prayers.
- Throw a party and play the music that they loved.
- Paint a picture using colors that reflect how you are feeling.
- Remember them in your journal.

- Light a candle in their memory.
- Volunteer with a charity or group that was special to your loved one.
- Establish a scholarship fund in their memory.
- Go on a photography walk and take pictures of things that remind you of your loved one.
- Plant a flower garden in a container or in your yard.
- Share a bouquet of flowers with someone who is sick or lonely.
- Sit and visit with someone who needs a friend.
- Write your loved one's name or something special about them on a smooth river stone. Keep it in a special place and hold it close to you when you are feeling sad.
- Spend time with your family or friends . . . laugh, cry, and share stories.
- Practice deep and relaxing breathing.
- Exercise.
- Be kind to yourself.

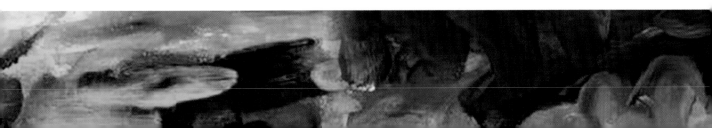

Resources on Grief and Loss

For children:

National Alliance for Grieving Children: childrengrieve.org

Children's Grief Education Association: childgrief.org

Sesame Street: www.sesamestreet.org/content/grief

New York Life—A Child in Grief: www.newyorklife.com/achildingrief

Rainbows for Children: rainbows.org

For everyone:

The Centering Corporation: centeringcorp.com

The Compassionate Friends: compassionatefriends.org

Grief Digest: griefdigestmagazine.com

Grief Healing: griefhealing.com

Living With Loss magazine: bereavementmag.com

GriefWork: www.osms.org/ministries/griefwork

The Jewish Bereavement Project: jewishbereavement.org

Association for Pet Loss and Bereavement: aplb.org

What's Your Grief?: whatsyourgrief.com

Surviving Life After a Parent Dies: slapd.com

American Foundation for Suicide Prevention: afsp.org

AfterTalk: aftertalk.com

Acknowledgments

This book is very special to me and would not have happened without the encouragement and support of some very special people.

Mr. Shelby and Mr. Gingles—high school art teachers—you saw something special in a sensitive and quirky teenager and encouraged him to find the artist within.

Terri Godfrey—a teacher and potter—through the ancient Japanese technique of pit firing raku pottery, you taught me that colors shine brighter after going through something as destructive and life-giving as fire. This wisdom has carried me through some pretty hard life lessons.

Those who have joined me around *The Painting Table*—your stories of grief and healing have touched me and changed me.

Phil Fox Rose, my editor, and the inimitable team at Paraclete Press—thank you for honoring my words and my art—and dreaming this beautiful book into reality.

Riley—I love you, my sweet girl. You have grown into an amazing young woman. The greatest honor ever bestowed on me is the honor of being your dad.

Kristin—as my wife and best friend, you've gifted me with your strength, encouragement, and boundless joy. You have filled my world with vibrant colors that have yet to be named, and you have loved me more than the stars in the sky.

Thank you . . . I love you.

Also Available from Paraclete Press . . .

Grieving: A Beginner's Guide

JERUSALEM HULL MCCORMACK

ISBN 978-1-55725-493-1 | $14.99 Paperback

This book is designed to help those in pain—and specifically those who are coping with how to grieve the death of a loved one—to imagine the path before them.

"Chances are, if you are reading this, your heart is broken. This book is designed to help those in pain—and specifically those who have lost someone through death—to imagine the path before them. It is a path of suffering. But it is also a path that may lead to unexpected discoveries—and to peace."
—Jerusha Hull McCormack

Available through your local bookseller or through Paraclete Press:
www.paracletepress.com; 1-800-451-5006